Kalakuta Republic

Chris Abani

Kalakuta Republic

Introduction by
Kwame Dawes

Saqi Books

British Library Cataloguing-in-Publication Data
A catalogue record for this book is available from the
British Library

ISBN 0 86356 973 0 (hb)
ISBN 0 86356 322 8 (pbk)

Saqi Books
26 Westbourne Grove
London W2 5RH
www.saqibooks.com

For
John James, cellmate, friend, brother,
tortured to death, June 1991, aged 14

and
Obioma Nzerem, Valentine Alily, Jacob Ross,
kindred spirits, dreamers, fools.

Acknowledgements

There is no way I can thank those who gave their lives so that I could live to tell this story. But there are people I can thank. Kwame Dawes and Bernardine Evaristo for their generosity, and critical and editorial feedback. Jacob Ross for initiating me into the final levels of my craft. Adrian Dutton for the amazing paintings that began it all and for the opportunity to be part of Still Dancing. My family for supporting me always – my mother Daphne and siblings Mark, Charles, Gregory and Stella. My father Michael, whose inability to understand me has led me to seek deeper and better ways of saying things. Pamela Osuji for always being there. Jillian Tipene for her help in developing my reading and performance skills and for that special friendship. Victor Okigbo for my first lessons in the art of poetry in 1987. Adam Pretty whose craft and patience in teaching me the saxophone has changed the rhythms of my writing. Delphine George who has made me a believer again. Helena Igwebuike and all my friends. John Moser and David Rose – men of honour. Juris Iven and *deus ex machina* in Brussels, without whom I might be dead. Patrick Galvin, Pat Boran and everyone in The Republic of Ireland – especially the Dublin posse. Harold Pinter, Moris Farhi, everyone at Saqi Books for believing, and everyone who has helped and supported me in the development of this work and my art in general – you all know who you are – thank you.

Contents

Author's Note

This collection of poetry is based around my experience as a political prisoner in Nigeria between 1985 and 1991. My first experience of this was the result of the publication of my first novel when I was sixteen. Two years after publication, in 1985, I was arrested as my novel was considered to be the blueprint for the foiled *coup* of General Vatsa. I was detained initially for six months, in two-three-month stretches. Released, I hid the details of my arrest from my family. This initial brush with the government was not deliberate on my part, but having once been brushed by the wings of the demon, I became a demon hunter. In 1987, when I entered university, I joined a guerrilla theatre group which performed plays in front of public buildings and government offices. The government wasted no time in re-arresting me. This time I was held for a year in Kiri Kiri maximum security prison.

In that year, I came to question everything I had believed in before. The only thing I never gave up on was the conviction that there can be no concession in the face of tyranny and oppression. I also learnt how truly ephemeral our mortality is. Released with no explanation, I returned to university and between studying for my degree in literature and developing my love of jazz, I wrote a play for the 1990 convocation ceremony for the university. The play, Song of a Broken Flute, led to my third and final period of incarceration for eighteen months, six of which were spent in solitary confinement. I was sentenced to death for treason – without trial – and held on death row with murderers, rapists and other convicted criminals.

In the last eighteen months, I shared a cell with a fourteen year old boy, John James, and twenty other men. John James did not leave Kiri Kiri alive. And there were many others. I have tried to represent those men and boys that I met, including the guards, as best as I can, without idealising anyone. The most difficult thing about my whole experience was not being able to share my pain, having to hide it from my family for their own protection and from my selfish need not to be talked out of doing the things I felt I had to.

And now? Every day is a careful balance fought between the despondency that threatens to swamp me and the incredible joy of living. I think that my art, my poetry, prose and music come from these cracks in my being, these ley lines where spirit is said to reside. I have come out of the horror of that experience having lost my faith in the inherent goodness of humanity, yet curiously appreciating even more the effort it takes to be good. I also kicked a bad smoking habit! If in reading these poems you can see the courage of the men and boys I write about, if you can feel their essential humanity, and realise that the best things in us cannot die, then I will have succeeded.

But remember always, that freedom, love, kindness, honour, justice and truth are never to be taken for granted – but worked at, struggled with and fought for, at whatever cost. For it is this that makes us human and builds a bridge to our true nature, which is spirit.

Baraka Bashad

Chris Abani
London, June 1997

Introduction

The alchemy of transforming terrible tragedies of human experience into art, into music, poetry, dance, sculpture, film can be an unforgiving vocation. Human tragedy is naturally compelling and the telling of human pain has always had an insidious attraction for human beings; yet after a while, a tale poorly told will grow tiresome and the listener numb to its details, to the pain. Such tales tend to fade away, to be put aside. The ones that last are those that transcend the pain. Yet, for the artist, a strange conflict remains, for if the artist has suffered, if the artist has seen the brute behaviour of other human beings inflicted on him, if the artist has felt the blows of another's hand on his or her body, blows meted out as punishment for some noble act, some act of righteous and moral defiance, some act of ideological fortitude, he or she does not want the art to be read simply as art, as something that transcends the details of its history, the details of the moment, the details of the cause. How do craft and content meet, how do passion and the ordered consideration of craft work hand in hand? How does one speak politics and yet contemplate such articulations as art? To answer such questions, we must assume that the artist is an artist regardless of where he or she finds him or herself. The artist will define his or her existence largely on the compulsion of making something extraordinary out of the mundane – it is a terrible compulsion that the artist avoids and ignores at his or her own peril. If this is true, then the artist will sing anyway, and will find ways of making song regardless of what the song is about. But not everyone succeeds in dealing with the conundrum of content and craft. Not all artists find the aesthetic that allows them to treat the political convulsions of these last hundred years in ways that do not make us question the very validity or relevance of art. But a handful have managed to make us believers – believers in the power of craft.

This month, I was drawn into the simple dialectics of four different artists – four poets from different times and places, all of them working their way through this dilemma of content and craft, and each emerging with songs of such beauty and force that they make me a believer. I was teaching Wilfred Owen's 'Dulce et Decorum Est' to a first year English class, and as we began to explore the tragedy that he describes and the strong polemic of his message, I began to feel that there was something almost callous about the stylistic control exercised in the crafting of this poem. For this poem is one of impeccable rhetoric – the rhetoric forged by structure, by form; and yet straining against this control, this order is this incredible and angry narrative of a brute and ugly death – a certain nightmarish reality that crawls in and out of the frame, but seems compelled to return always to the safety of the frame. It was here that I began to see an answer, that the poet turned to form, turned to the ordering of verse to manage the disorder of his vision of a fellow soldier drowning in a sea of noxious gases. The craft was his saviour, his calming moment. The craft allowed him to speak, to determine a discourse of ideas, a discourse that would emerge as a polemic, but a deeply musical polemic. Yet this was not enough for me. I still had not answered the question of whether this poem shone purely on the basis of its gruesome and realistic content, its emotive surface, or whether it was art in essence. I was not sure that the poem's success did not rest on Owen's special access to suffering. But was I using a misguided paradigm of art?

My attempt to define the Blues aesthetic to students on another course offered me a way to understand this dialogue between art and suffering, art and pain, art and politics. The Blues is first form and then passion. The form is powerful, compelling and heavily present, compelling the artist to work within a framework that maintains a fairly constant template for which experience must must be shaped. Prompted by smart people like Houston Baker, Amiri Baraka, Langston Hughes and Kalamu ya Slaam, it occurred to me that the act of formalising experience, the business of taking pain and making it into something manageable, something that comes under the control of the artist and then the listener, is the fundamental aesthetic shared by people who write out of suffering. I saw then that perhaps I write out of a need to find order in the midst of disorder, driven by the compulsion of self-preservation. It is cathartic because one is busy imposing something like order on the chaos of existence, and in doing this, one is giving life to the moment, to the experience one is managing. The Blues triumphs not because it is a clever song, but because it is. The very existence of the Blues represents the moment of craft, the moment of artistic expressions and the moment of possibility. It offers a way to cope with reality; as Ma Rainey argues, in August Wilson's play about her, 'You sing 'cause that's a way of understanding "life".' She continues, 'The Blues help you get out of bed in the morning. You get up knowing you ain't alone. There is something else in the world. Something's being added by that song. This would be an empty world without the Blues. I take that emptiness and try to fill it up with something.' Here, what is being celebrated is the art piece, the finished crafted piece. It never changes the void, but it fills the void.

And so even when a poet like Bob Marley tries to chart a path of righteousness for the nations, even as he attempts to be a prophet, declaring, predicting, preaching, praying, worshipping in his songs, we are unable to avoid the fact that all of this is riding a rhythm, locked into a form that is tight and steady, that is comforting and a safe place in the chaos. His declaration in 'Trench Town Rock' is perhaps then his most profound and most decisive articulation of his craft: 'One good thing about music, when it hits, you feel no pain'. It is not so much what it teaches, but what it fills, and how it manages to touch us in ways that are only explained by the beauty of the crafting of the words. To teach this to students is sometimes difficult for they want answers, they are not always interested in finding a salve for souls through the music of words placed beside each other or the tenor of the sounds that emanate from the sound system in the lecture hall. I would have to lead them into a dancehall and let the music consume them. I would have to assure them that sometimes just hearing the words emerge and carry their own music is enough to say that you have understood, even if you have not grasped the poem, its semantics, its 'meaning'. These three preoccupations, with Owen's war poetry, the Blues and with Marley's reggae prepared me to read and read again the poetry of Chris Abani. For Abani has written a series of poems that present us with some fundamental questions that go to the heart of the meaning of this word art.

The poems in *Kalakuta Republic* are not the first poems by Chris Abani I have read. About two years ago, I was sent a thick bundle of poetry in preparation for a workshop I was going to do in London with groups of poets including Abani. I read his work quickly, noting the pieces that were strong and skimming quickly over others. I was looking for high points, moments of illumination, and above all for ticks, little habits that would annoy anyone who read poetry a great deal. Abani's verse was competent, at times strong, but not especially compelling. There was a kind of calm, a playfulness, flirting around promising ideas, but I was not comunicating with him as I read. I was skirting around a person, a voice, sensing obvious talent, but one without an agenda, nothing desperate in the work emerged. So it was a lesson to me when I read some months later the poems that would become part of the *Kalakuta Republic* anthology. I read the poems quickly and was shocked. I started to wonder about what was happening to me. My first reading suggested that these were stunning poems, but I quickly grew sceptical. I had to to ask myself what was moving me. Was it the content, the ideas, that I was staring into the graphic details of someone's incarceration? Was it because I was touching sheets by someone who had watched others die cruel and useless deaths? Was it because I felt no sense of authority to question even the whole business of poetry in the face of such themes? I also had to ask whether there would be anything wrong with being moved by the themes, the stories, the horrors. Would it be wrong, a compromise of art to say simply that the poems were good because they were about moving and tragic things? I allowed these questions to rest on my mind during the second and third readings. And when I turned to write to Chris, I had to take the poems one by one and find out what he was doing about transforming tragedy into art. How was he doing his Blues, his Reggae piece? I realised, the poems would soon lose their weight, their force, if their shock value was all that sustained them. So I returned to the manuscript and began to test, defying my awe of his pain, my tendency to be mesmerised and sometimes muted by his struggle. I asked him to think about cutting this or that, to add that or the other, despite the danger that I might be trampling on his nightmares and his memories. The reader of this collection will invariably be faced with the same challenge, for to approach this collection dispassionately would be inhuman, perhaps impossible. But there is something about the audacity of rendering experience into verse that requires something more from the poet. There is a tyranny that undergrids the poem, which rests in this notion of craft. The poem must exist for its own sake. What a daunting challenge.

It is especially gratifying to be able to say that by the time Chris Abani was through his multiple nightmares with the making of these poems, he had emerged with a work made up of graceful pieces of art, almost ready to be hung in a gallery for others to come and enter them and rest and weep in them, and to admire.

The narrative of Chris Abani's encounter with the military system that inflicted itself on him, as it has on thousands of other Nigerians, is a disturbing one, and eloquently captured by the poems in this collection. The details of Abani's several arrests, his efforts to be a voice of protest in Nigeria and the suffering that he went through as a result of these imprisonments are outlined in fittingly sardonic prose at the beginning of the collection, witness to his capacity to manage his struggle with wit and honesty. It is the honesty of the individual trying to fathom the motivation for martyrdom, the motivation for being a young rebel who will then be shocked into incarceration and encounters with death, and it is powerfully evoked. Abani's capacity to suggest that there is a quest for some kind of fame through even legitimate protest renders the experience frighteningly true, for it confesses a secret of those who lead in struggles, it confesses that there is an ego that walks hand in hand with the generosity of protest. The meeting of the ego and the suffering – the degradation of imprisonment and pure abuse – represents one of the most striking and moving elements of this collection. These nuances recovered from the memory of watching others die and Abani's own time in confinement or in that notorious coffin of a box, represent the heart of the poetry of this collection. There is nothing more poignant than the brief dialogue that ends the frenzied orgy of murder in the poem 'Mango Chutney', so tidily drawn in those two-line stanzas of almost courtly finesse, belying the shock of the subject matter:

I never get used to the amount of
blood; bodies droop like so many flowers.

Eyes stare, bright and alive into
another world. And death becomes some men.

The same composure that ends the poem is that of deep and disturbing pain, the composure of confession that must be ordered and organised within the safety of the poem if the poet is to find a possibility for redemption:

'Who did they shoot tonight?' a cell mate asks.
'I don't care' I reply looking away. 'As long as it's not me.'

Daily epiphanies bloom as angels walk among us;
the few, the chosen.

To admit in this moment that he, asked by an older man to write their story in blood, is not an angel, and yet that he walks among angels is to subsume the ego and to allow the poem to be an anthem for the angels, for the many that people the poem – those that died in jail, those that never saw the outside world. It also evokes the sadness of the survivor who has no good answer for why he has survived. In this, Abani's poem works its way through the complexities of the theme and emerges in song, rich and powerful.

I have read the work of other poets who have written about their lives in jail. Sadly many of them have been Africans: Soyinka, Brutus, Awoonor et al. This is rich and noble company. It is company that may comfortably be joined by a poet like Yusef Komounyakaa, the brilliant American whose poems about his time in Vietnam admirably represent the genre of art emerging out of the crisis of human existence. All these unquestionably great writers have discovered that the poem about suffering is really one about finding beauty in suffering. The poem about incarceration is really a poem about freedom. The fact is that the poem, by its very nature, defies the baseness of suffering. By becoming the vehicle for the expression of horror, the poem forces the horror to be something else, to be managed, to be transformed into something beautiful. It is the '*dulce*' in Owen's poem, it is the soul, the heart, the pulse in Marley's songs; it is the perfection of the Blues, the comfort and predictability of its verse by verse punch-lines. Abani's poetry manages to understand this quality in poetry, and in the midst of his remembrances of the prison we sense that he is, for the moment, finding a ray of light, something like distraction in the art of verse – a way to escape the madness and the tragedy through these poems.

For us, the result is some very fine poetry. There is a sensibility at work here that promises us these will not be the only poems he will write. It is an instinct for the well-wrought line, the care to make an image work, the instinct for metaphor and an understanding of the importance of carefully honed and rendered sentiment. But the future is not something we can easily predict. This collection represents a splendid introduction to what we tend innocuously to call a poet of great promise. Abani's work emerges out of his strong Nigerian roots, and his writing is properly tied to other Nigerian and African writers. Yet, there is an expansiveness to his vision that allows his work to resonate with meaning beyond the confines of Kalakuta. In exile, there is distance that allows for memory that remains painful to be controlled. Always below the surface is the pain of the political situation in Nigeria, the memory of the deaths, the memory of his own fear, the residual nightmares of his life – they are all there, brimming beneath the surface like tears held in. Sometimes, as we read, we find ourselves scratching too deep and the salt seeps out. There is something noble and touching in this, something that makes us angry at the terrible politics of *coups* and dictatorships and by which we are amazed at the resilience and possibilities of the artist in that space. Abani's poems eschew any discourse on ideologies – he does not want to reduce the moments of his poems to polemic, and perhaps the prison term has scraped away the ideologies, replacing them with another kind of vocation – the raw and simple vocation of the artist searching out words. Maybe this is the result of suffering, or of the disillusionment felt by many engaged African writers, or even of greater disillusionment experienced by the younger Nigerian poets whose ideological preoccupations have been complicated by the chaos that permeates their existence in Nigeria. Whatever it is, this is a fresh voice and one that needs to be listened to. For this alone, I regard *Kalakuta Republic* as an important work. What Abani will do with the experience of creating these well-crafted poems remains to be seen. But one senses that there is much in a poet who manages to end his collection with the kind of control and sense of timing that we see in 'Jacob's Ladder'.

> . . . yet you are afraid
> to proceed more than a few
>
> steps from the gate. Convinced you
> will be shot in the back.
>
> Or that people will recoil from you
> knowing you carry the stench
> of death on your paler skin.
> But nothing happens.
>
> A gentle breeze ruffles your shirt and
> a dog menaces a parked car.
>
> The smell of frying plantain
> carried gently hurts inexplicably.
>
> Cold, sweet Coca-Cola stings you
> to tears.

Kwame Dawes
Columbia, SC, 1997

Portal

Dark waters of the beginning.

Rays, violet and short, piercing the gloom,
foreshadow the fire that is dreamed of.

Christopher Okigbo
Heavensgate

Portal

When first arrested
18.
Excited by possibilities of fame;
inflamed by
legends of political prisoners: sure that
Amnesty would free me.

But the days
dragged
into months;
no charge
no sign
of camera-toting journalists
from Reuters;
no word
from my family;
no amnesty.

Caught in the cross-hairs of fear,
the only way to mark
the days is by counting the beatings
3 a day
62 days: 186.

Housed in comfort; relative to;
I watch the trials on TV of
my co-conspirators; stomach fisted
waiting
my turn.
But they are too embarrassed to try me.

6 months later
unable to hold me any longer and
no doubt alarmed
at how much it
costs
to feed me; they give in
I am free to go.

II

1987,
deciding to take them on
I
stand
daily; reciting their crimes in epics
daring them: 'Go on. Kill me. Make me famous.'

They do
But 20 is not 18
Guns, boots, truncheons, knuckles
I realise – too late –
this time it's for real
I've had my dress rehearsal.

Pain draws out time razor sharp
but I am unbeaten;
I martyr my anger
profaning their idolatrous power
again;
straight to jail; I do not pass go.

Shovelling
with three fingers cold corn porridge
into my mouth,
the enormity of it:
I am being held by killers
and nobody knows I'm here.

Kiri Kiri
Maximum Security prison
D wing; or E, I forget
with the worst of the head cases:
Fela Anikulapo Kuti
smiling: 'Truth, my young friend is a risky business.'

I wish to be kept informed of your new publications and events

Subjects in which I have a special interest

☐ Art & Architecture ☐ History ☐ Politics ☐ Anthropology
☐ Women's Studies ☐ Fiction ☐ Poetry ☐ Languages

Other interests: ....

Name ....

Address ....

....

Postcode .... Country ....

E-mail ....

Your requests can also be sent by e-mail to: saqibooks@dial.pipex.com

Saqi Books
26 Westbourne Grove
London W2 5RH
United Kingdom

Mask

Fearing
they would be hurt,
or used to blackmail
me, I
never once asked to
see,
speak,
visit,
telephone

my family
cannot know.

This lie,
worn
to the softness of a favourite shirt
disintegrates when I touch it.
These are not images
to make you happy.

Or sad, or cry, or laugh
just a reminder that
tyranny stalks
us.

Old Warrior

One night
    a week after he arrived
he crawled across the cell

    and shook
      me
      awake.

'Please call me papa'
    he begged.
'60 years I have been somebody's
      papa.
I must have someone to be papa
      to.'

So a few of us called
    him Papa Joe until
      he died.

Rasa*

For Fela Anikulapo Kuti

A regular. Nicknamed 'Customer',
he even renamed his house Kalakuta Republic,

to honour the death
of conscience,

to ridicule them, those despots
swollen by their putrescence.

He had a saxophone smuggled into
jail and on some nights

riffed out a forlorn blues
condensing the walls into hot tears.

And we believed the notes wove
themselves into a terror that carried

on the wind, disturbing evil's sleep.

---

* Literally juice. It also refers to an emotional state; in music it is the
soul of performance. The fifth Veda describes *rasa* as a permanent
mood experienced by the audience conveyed only by a musician
who has experienced *rasa*. There are nine *rasas*: love, laughter, rage,
pathos, terror, disgust, heroism, wonder and tranquility.

Oyinbo Pepper*

I tried to intervene
in a fight once. They
rounded on me:
'Oyinbo pepper', one taunted pushing me.
'No more colonialism, fool!'

Later I asked Turko why.
'Why what?'
'Why do they resent me? Am I not here with them?'
'But you don't have to be. Won't always be. And
when this is over, you can go to England or America.
   Start
again. It's not you they resent, it's not having a choice
that burns them up'

* Sunburned whitey.

Chain Reaction

Prison psychiatrist
from Harvard.
Not completely
insensitive, starts his programme gently.
A dog is brought inside; intending ROW X
to nurture it.

That night
we hear its pitiful chained whines.
A thud, then silence broken only by
the crackle of a fire.

Morning scatters
ash from a makeshift hearth
patterning strewed gnawed bones,
stirring the chain to empty chink.

Ahimsa*

My assailant does not
seem capable of this sadism.
Tortoiseshell glasses
perched on nose tip, softens
even the most brutish face into intelligence.

He kicks me repeatedly; unprovoked.
I cough blood onto the ground to
stop from choking. His boot on my
neck forces me to take mouthfuls of mud.

Beatings have a rhythm.
Once your body learns it, the
pain loses its edge, smudging
ink-stained over your mind. But
they watch for the loss of focus in your eyes.

Seeing this, he reaches down
and pushes his revolver into my
mouth. I tense, my waiting spreading
wetly into the sand.
Suddenly there is a shout from my left shoulder.

---

*   *Ahimsa* is the Hindu–Jani religious practise of not harming any living
     thing.

Straining, I see a young guard,
Edward, pointing his rifle at
my assailant. 'Leave him now or I shoot you!'
he barks. 'Leave him. What
kind of animal are you. Bastard!' He rams

a bullet into the breach. I spit out oily
metal as my assailant stands up. He smiles,
'You will learn. You'll see. You will learn'.
But Edward, helping me to my feet
is not listening.

Passion Fruit

Here

Sex is not always a choice
lovingly made and enjoyed like
plump well-handled self-chosen fruit
teeth sinking into soft flesh in a dribble of pleasure.

Nevertheless
it abounds.

Some because it is the
truth of their being.

Some to deny, negate, sate
deep yearning, wordless, timeless.

Even the most rabid homophobe
can give in
to gentle caresses
comfort in this loveless, concrete
cesspit.

Some never do
and not from fear and loathing.

Some erupt in
painful, bloody, self-annihilating rape.

Some fall in
love; soft green moss caressing crumbling walls.

Some, unable to stomach
the truth that all love is light
amputate their own penes, laughing insanely
as they bleed to a stump.

Concrete Memories

In an empty cell,
stone
worn
tortured
scalded
by tides
of warm blood
and water,
petrifies their guilt.

Nicknamed
Kalakuta Republic
in some distant pain
by inmate or guard.
Techniques to extract confessions:
tried, tested, proven.
Interrogations are carried out.

Teeth,
pulled from their roots
with rusty pliers.
Methodical, clinical; each
raw tender wound
disinfected by gentle cigarette embers
and rubbing alcohol
mixed with salt for extra bite.

Rusty
cold
barrel of Winchester
bolt-action Mark IV rifle;
retired right
arm of imperialism.
Enema. Rammed
up rectum, repeatedly;
twirling cocktail
swizzle-stick.
Extremely effective, they say
at dislodging caked-in conspiracies.

Tequila Sunrise

Angola beer. Brewed to perfection.
Only the best ingredients are used.

Reward for those daring to reject any act
that jars with their sensibilities; moralities.

Equal part water

and steaming urine.

Bets placed. Dares. How many bottles can they force

down your throat

before you

a) gag
b) choke
c) die.

This is not

a game for warders,

but for fellow prisoners, peers
friends; an excellent ice breaker.

Roll Call

I remember rising one night
after midnight
and moving
through an impulse of loneliness
to try and find the stars.

Dennis Brutus
Letters to Martha

Job

1900
hours
cramped together: now
20 men in a cell built for 8.

Space is a closely fought ideal,
savagely defended prize.

Two men smoking:
'If you die tonight can I have your shirt?'
'Sure. If you do, I want your pencil.'

Job. Older than any of us
remembers
this prison run by British soldiers.

'Let me die. Please let me die', he cries.
No one replies. No one will console him.

Here death is courted. Welcomed.
Not in defeat. Or cowardice,
but as a statement
of our

Discontent
with this state of barbarism we
live
Under

the shade of a tree
executions are mercifully shielded
from the harsh sun.

Killing Time

1900
hours.

Killing time. 12. Anointed.
Blindfolded. Herded by seraphs
wings tinged rusty by innocent blood.

Stapled
to a pock-marked wall by fear
steel bolts, ratchet bullets.

Shots crack

like so many branches.
Of 12, 8 fall.
Shirt, pencil and all.

I know I am alive
because
terror drips down my legs.

Jeremiah

Jeremiah
     was 6 feet, 9 inches the last
time we measured.

Face,
     knotted against
sun-hard pain,

unravels.
     Smiles, spread hemp
tendrils.

Often
     fasting, he passes his food to
weaker, needier men.

He
     stood between guards and a prone man,
helping him up

to
     die on his feet, knees only slightly
        buckled, eyes kissing the sun.

The Box

Wooden frame with skirt of sheet metal
6 foot by 3 foot by 3 foot.

Pin-pricks of air burn holes on the negative
of my body; choking on my own smell mingled
with scent of seared hair and skin,
I taste my pungent mortality.

One hour later:

Religion unfurls in desperate splendour.
Silently through old man's mumbling lips
prayers tumble forth; spells to keep the
terror at bay; currency to buy salvation.

Matthew, Mark, Luke and John
bless this bed that I lie on.
Before I lay my head to sleep
I beg thee Lord, my soul to keep.

Two hours later:

Fear cramps me into panic; hysterical
I beat frantically, futilely at the sides.
2 inches is inadequate leeway; I only
brand dull thumps onto taut knuckles.

Three hours later:

Counting out time on beads of sweat
to keep from going insane. Mental
arithmetic. 2678 divide by the pie of 7.
Nursery rhymes work also – except when tears
muffle memory.

Four hours later:

Blank face, blank black eyes stare; icy
dense darkness; free falling, nothing below
except inky space sucking me into maw.
These are some of my nameless terrors.

Five hours later:

Water is thrown over the metal to cool me.
Through burning steam I see
a man in dazzling robes; face, a thousand suns
coming towards me; leading to light . . .

Six hours later:

'. . . Jesu, Jesu, Jesu . . .'
chants bubble through blisters.
'Poor devil', someone in the cell mutters
'Shut up fool!' another snarls.

Someone else, too impatient
to reach the hole in the floor
stands arms akimbo
spattering my face with urine.

'Thank you, thank you . . .' I mumble
as the hot ammonia stings me

into life.

Eden

Burping fumes and stenches
we squelch through the swamp to
the clearing in the centre.

Bubbling mud cauldron sighs contentedly
displacing corpses; hands scratching weeds,
smiles – green, brown – sludged.

We settle down to work under eyes
of guards smoking, hunched in shade,
vultures picking the bones of our pain.

In pairs we throw bodies into the shallow
pit along with vomit.

And the swamp sucks our feet in sleep,
dreaming us into wet intestines; waking
us, screaming, sweating.

People will do anything to get out of
graveyard shift. One man drops a heavy
concrete block crunching toes to mush.

But they hobble him along with a spade.
'. . . before you join dem dere . . .' they
threaten nicely, not forgetting to say please.

The stench, guilt, burnt into nostrils never leaves
you hugging cloying cheap cologne on a hot day
that will not wash away.

Paper Doll

Christiana we call him,
this caricature who wears
prison shorts torn into a skirt and stains
himself with plant dye.

Fluttering at anyone who pays
attention he offers to suck cock
for ten cigarettes, fuck for thirty.
Anything else costs from five packs up.

'It's not that I like to sell myself cheap,' she told
me one night, smoke rings mugging her.
'It is just that I have to keep busy, you see,
because idle hands is the devil's workshop.'

Tattoo

Saddam.

Even the guards call me that. Few people
want to know my real name.

Here

Everybody goes by an alias.
Perhaps it is to avoid intimacy.

Dangerous

when you might be burying your
best friend the next day, or

Superstitious

belief we can evade
death and the guards, live just one hour longer.

Perhaps

we believe we are protecting family
afraid that they might also pay for our dreaming.

JJ,

Kojo, Mambo, Kingfisher, Vampire,
Lucifer, Echo, Tango, Akula, even Coltrane

Hide

behind these facades. I play the game
too. John James knows my real name.

Invisibility

stalks our every step. Some men brand,
with cashew sap, their names on buttocks, stomachs,

Hidden

from view. A welt to remind them of
who they really are, their past, their only hope.

An English Gentleman

Mixed race parentage can have
its advantages here.

Smiled sweetly in an
English accent

'Good afternoon Sir. Did you want
me to join the execution line?'

Often guarantees reprieve, a hasty
'Not you. You are a gentleman.'

Some treat me with disdain, call me 'bat'
Neither of sky, nor ground.

Others defer to me, carrying over the belief
that any hint of whiteness is next to godliness.

Some are indifferent, treating me like a
prisoner on death row. Ruthlessly.

To some I am a rabid vampire feeding
on their humiliation.

Territorial even in suffering.

Waiting for Godot

Jeremiah on death row,
has not been tried – or formally charged.

But it's only been seven years. He is
an infant 'awaitee'. He

killed a soldier who shot his
seven-year-old son for breaking a window

with an errant football.

John James is teaching him to read
from stolen Marvel comics, newspapers and pages

ripped from Enid Blyton and Biggles.

With lights-out comes the silence,
predatory, malevolent.

Echoing comfortingly, the sound of Jeremiah
straining words through shrouded candlelight

like seeds through a sieve.

'What's up, Spidey?'

'Damn, I've run out of
webbing.'

'Jerry at four o'clock, Biggles.'

'Oh no, it's the Cloaked Crusader!'

Casual Banter

Sergeant Adamu Barkin Zawa
rammed the barrel

of a rifle – Lee Enfield – up my rectum
maintaining casual banter;

'How is your mother? How is she
finding our lovely country?' interrupted only
by the blood spraying from my backside,

baptising his heavily scarified face,
empty ancient mask.

Breath heavy with local gin – ogogoro – used
to scare demons, guilt, into lonely
dark corners.

Haunted by screams,
John James dying shamelessly,

he sits under the moon howling, torn apart.
Compassion cups my hands through the bars
to try and console,

or is it kill,
this man.

Sergeant Adamu, decorated murderer of Biafra,
specialising in women, children.

We find him leashed to the execution tree
by leather army-issue belt,
smelling faintly

of mangoes.

Boddhisatva*

There are others . . .

Lieutenant Hyacinth Leviticus Nwankwo.
Officer in charge of torture and
interrogations, self-appointed redeemer.

'What does it profit a man to gain
the whole world but lose his soul?'
he asks, coaxing confessions with a pair of pliers.

'If your right arm causes you to sin . . .'
he intones as his machete butters
through flesh too surprised to bleed.

Or flogging, bull whip burning Satan,
he drives the demons from
this holy sanctuary, the Lord's temple.

'Do not die in sin,' he urges those
too hard to break or who have nothing to say.
'Accept Jesus as your personal saviour.'

* Buddhist. Enlightened being. Teacher of faith.

Other times, he sits in, watching
his many apprentices practise detailed
knowledge of human anatomy

while mumbling prayers,
fingering a rosary made from the teeth of
his favourite dead prisoners.

Koro*

Sodomites row.
Dreaded more than the box; or
solitary.

Hyacinth Leviticus Nwankwo's
favourite punishment, supervised
personally,

is to leave some hapless new
prisoner overnight in these cells,
not forgetting

to spread the rumour that he is
a rampant sodomite with a touch
of sadomasochism thrown in for flavour.

We can hear the screams clear
across the courtyard, even with dirt
stuffed in our ears.

* Yoruba slang for dark alley.

Mephistopheles

Lt Emile Elejegba loved nothing more
than a good debate about
who was the better writer: Zola or Balzac.

And did Dostoyevsky not plagiarise
St John and Revelations a little too much
As against Tolstoy's more original ideas?

Plato and Artistotle he maintained
stole all their concepts from Yoruba mythology
or else were illegitimate children of Oduduwa.

He hated Kiri Kiri and the brutality,
but was posted here, demoted, as
punishment for his refusal to

lead a troop into Ogoniland to
murder fellow compatriots. Back
then he was a captain.

I was summoned often to his office
to do 'paper-work'. He would
leave me alone to get on with it

After cautioning me not to read
under any circumstances the copy of
Anna Karenina on his desk.

Good Friday

Day burnt down to purple embers,
fanned by egrets, unrolling black velvet.

Sounds of night vault the high walls
falling in loud heaps at our feet to be

kicked aside as we shuffle to dinner,
black eyed beans, stale yam, boll weevils.

I shunt the tasteless food,
crunching noisily on the weevils, listening to

John James and Jeremiah arguing about
X-Men and Apocalypse, goodies vs arch-villains.

'But why fight a foe you can never beat.
It seems futile to me', Jeremiah argued.

'It does not matter whether you win in the
short run. What is important is that you fight.'

'Isn't that right?' John James asks me.
I nod absently, distracted.

I wish I had paid more attention that night. Those were the last words John James spoke to me.

They took him in the morning. Three days later, on his birthday, he died. Smoked to nothingness.

Ode to Joy

John James, 14,
refused to serve his conscience up
to indict an innocent man.
Handcuffed to chair, they tacked his penis
to the table
with a six inch nail
and left him there

to drip
to death
3 days later.

Risking death, an act insignificant
in the face of this child's courage,
we sang:

Oje wai wai,
Moje oje wai, wai.

Incensed,
they went
on a
killing rampage.

Guns
knives
truncheons

even canisters of tear gas,
fired close up or
directly into mouths, will
take the back
of
your head off
and many men
died singing
that night.

Notes caught
surprised,
suspended
as blows bloodied mouths,
clotting into silence.

Caliban

Fear grows on you,
smooth like well worn trouser buttocks.

Inmates devise elaborate schemes to
keep from being released, because

after twenty years in hell, heaven is too
terrible a possibility to contemplate.

Akula in cell block H, the deadliest men,
cannot live on the outside. He kills and

eats nearly all his room-mate. The guards find him
picking his teeth with small finger.

They kill him slowly, cutting him up piece
by piece, forcing him to eat himself.

The Hanged Man

Owusu
is not even a Nigerian.
He came from Ghana looking
for work.

The foreman
at a construction site,
a corpulent Igbo, asked to
sleep with his sister
as a reference.

Having no relatives near
he produced his girlfriend.
'Why?' I asked incredulously
'She love me,' he smiled.

Classic story. Someone stole some
tools. The foreigner was
fingered. Kiri Kiri next stop.

Receiving advance notice of
his impending death he
pulled out his solid gold tooth by
tying string to it and
slamming a door.

Handing the still bleeding tooth
to me, he asks me to
have it made into a ring for his
girlfriend.

'Give her – she has a son for me.'
I nod, tears tracking the dirt on my face.
'Make sure you give her.'
Again, I nod.
'Pray for me,' he whispers urgently.
'I don't want to have lived in vain.'

He died a week later.
I did not know his surname
or where to find his girlfriend.

And anyway, Sargeant Adamu found
the gold tooth when
his rifle dislodged it from my
anus.

Buffalo Soldier

In the last week before
he died, John James would cry softly
every night.

His father, colonel on the wrong side
absconded to Chad, across the border –
they came looking for him.

Finding only John James and his mother,
they took him, ransom for his father's head;
but he never came – maybe he never knew.

Unable to lose face, they held JJ anyway;
one extra hand for graveyard duty – and practise
for artists seeking the perfect torture.

This child's only crimes were an overactive
imagination, a belief in the unseen – a father who
haunted a despot.

He sucked, through eager eyes tales from Jeremiah:
goblins, ghosts, cannibals and parallel worlds. Doesn't
he recognise the plots from the comics he gave him?

In the week before
he died, John James' laughter fell
mauve gossamer blossoms from a tree shaking.

Heavensgate

The other politicos,
privileged by class,
education, family,

preen in their bravado,
safe from death, protected by old,
powerful benevolence.

They pay other inmates to sing their praises:
Shouts of 'Baba! Baba! Poor man's saviour'
chase their farts echoing up their own arses.

Other heroes here are men and boys
with no power, no privilege, no class,
nothing to gain: not even a book published.

Their crime is to be poor and proud
in the face of tyranny: unbroken by angels
they worry liars to madness.

And one of these nameless
crawled into my cell at night via sewer pipe
to give me a jar of his own blood

and paper, stolen inch by inch, hidden up
trained rectums and glued together into
sheets with mango sap.

'To take write our suffering'

These true heroes are lost
in the heat hazes that shimmer over unmarked
graves riddling the swamp behind the prison walls.

Mango Chutney

Plucking mangoes
Sport for guards, soldiers, policemen.

Drunk, home bound from shift-end
they stop at death row, choose casually,

lining us up against the wall scarred from
previous plucking, under that spreading tree.

Picking his teeth, Hassan, veteran of this
game, picks us off, shooting blindfolded.

Last rites, an unceremonious smoke
harsh, throat and lung burning.

Usually pure marijuana soaked in valium.
They aren't too good at moving targets.

Sometimes they tie us, binding to post.
Legs have a habit of giving out in the face of death,

knees kneading your shame into dust, your feet
muffling whimpers in the sand.

Tied there, you die in clockwork regularity
long before any shots are fired.

Guns spit, arcs of fire hit bodies,
jerking limbs drown in empty spaces.

Bullets dust your body apologetically; you slump
but hemp hugs tightly so only your head lolls

face hidden. Ropes cut fresh tribal marks onto
your body, weight pulling against them.

Untied, you crumble slowly to the floor, and leaves
fall in spirals to land on bloody corpses.

I never get used to the amount of
blood; bodies droop like so many flowers.

Eyes stare, bright and alive, into
another world. And death becomes some men.

Others wear it shamefully; others still, defiantly.
Their protest choking, suffocating.

Looking on, you notice small details.
His trousers are torn at the groin. He has a

lazy eye which gazes crookedly
into your mind.

His crime? Maybe he said no in the face of tyranny.
Maybe he murdered. The point? We will never know.

Walking over to the bodies, Hassan kicks them
hoping perhaps that they are not all dead.

The problem with mango plucking is the fruit
falls too quickly; and harvest season is over far too
    soon.

Spitting he bends down and cuts their throats
– to make doubly sure – vermin are tough and
    cunning.

Judge, jury, executioner – Hassan, drunken
petty tyrant; lust, rude and unbridled

by gun and 27 allocated rounds of ammo per week.
And for me a simple lust – to live as long as I can.

'Let's go,' he shouts to his friends; amid
much laughter and back slapping they leave.

'Who did they shoot tonight?' a cell mate asks.
'I don't care,' I reply looking away, 'as long as it's not
    me.'

Daily epiphanies bloom as angels walk among us,
the few, the chosen.

Rambo 3

October 1.
Independence Day.

As a special treat, reforming us
to accept this great nationhood

we are shown a film in the
dusty, dirty execution yard.

The killing wall serves as screen
old bullet wounds freckling the celluloid.

Those who can recite the national anthem offhand
get a free cola; throw in the pledge and you get a
    bun.

Hours before the film, the courtyard echoes the
voices of hungry men learning them in rote.

Rambo 3. We cheer as Stallone
achieves, in 3 hours, the impossible.

Defying and destroying fascism – But there is no
make-up, doughnuts for crew or fake blood here.

Prices are higher, time moving slower.
But then, we have terrible inflation.

Hearing us cheer at the chattering guns
on screen, explosions echoing our hope

and believing we are rioting,
a passing patrol storms the prison.

Sprayed like so much water from a hose,
bullets chase our fear across the courtyard.

Trampling shame and dignity underfoot,
blood runs thick with spilt cola.

'Eat this,' Stallone says repeatedly as
the dead projectionist's body jams the projector.

Later, the body count is high; over
one hundred are dead – or dying.

From my cell window, overturned chairs
check each other in a complex chess game.

Not the laughter, cheering, Coca-Cola
or Rambo 3 – not even the brief gasp of hope.

All I remember are the screams of men in agony,
the curious pop of exploding flesh, the stains on my
    shirt.

Passover

Before he was transferred
         again
for fraternising with the prisoners,

Lt Emile Elejegba came to
         see me
in my cell at night.

Wrinkling his nose against the
         smell
and trying hard not to cry,

he handed me a slim worn
         volume
with the picture of a smiling white girl
         on its cover. *The Diary of Anne Frank*.

'This might help,' he said gently.
    'I hear
Nelson Mandela read it on Robbens Island.'

In the morning he was gone as
    I turned
the first page and began to read.

Still Dancing

I anoint my heart
Within its flame I lay
Spent ashes of your hate –
Let evil die.

Wole Soyinka
I Anoint my Flesh

Birds of Paradise

Single

Window.

Through murky glass, outside glimpses.
No roses, hibiscus or bachelor's buttons are planted
    here.
But in insolent defiance, a bird of paradise

runs

amok

with colour. Screaming in ancient tongue
my spirit to fray.
Even pain cannot breach
my conviction that the best in us cannot die.

From

that window

sunlight
trembles in the musty air,
caressing my torturer's arm pausing him in

downward

blow.

Sweat blisters his face
and when the blow connects drawing blood,
spittle, broken teeth, it is

soft sweet

lover's embrace.

Square Dancing

Two prisoners face off in the courtyard
cheered on by a bored audience.

Sunlight diamonds off a piece of glass;
the other prisoner is unarmed.

Flesh is very fragile, ripped open,
it reveals a soft malleable matrix.

Blood, water, bones. Fabric tears:
Red jelly of a heart, pink clouds of lungs

knots of muscle. The glass sighs into
the other, drawing bubbling red blisters.

The others turn away, bored again.
And the unknown, unnamed prisoner

denied even a number, dies here.
The dust sucking life up indifferently.

Death does not always wear guards
uniforms, but it is always foretold.

With time, you acquire second sight,
the ability to smell its funk.

Stir-Fried Visions

Black-eyed beans again.
Popular because they ballast stomachs
to a healthy illusion which deflates
at first gas.

Okoro, practical joker,
stands beside the huge metal drums used
to cook and pretends to pee into the steaming beans.
The kitchen detail cracks up at the looks

on the faces of these
hard prisoners, men who would not balk
at murdering a child. When he died, no one
noticed for a week, believing it another prank.

There is the incredible self-awareness, deep bonds
between men, and the routine and monastic discipline
can be applied to many tasks, shaping our lives.

And sometimes, on a hot day, sweat crawling all
over you, tomb flies flaunting the stench everywhere:
searching for sense, seeing only random pebbles on
    a beach,
your mind cracks open and you glimpse paradise.

Egwu Onwa*

At night, squinting off to the left
      just so,
stars corral across the barbed wire
on top of the high walls.

---

*   Moon dance, a children's game. Also refers to a time of innocence.

Terminus

Last bus
stop.

End of
the line
for most,
leaving in cheap coffins
postmarked 'Return to Sender'.

Smoke Screen

Humour here swells, filling our nostrils.
Percolating senses. It is not bravery

in noble round-table tradition,
but the best disinfectant against death's rankness.

Laughter, square-wedged down our throats,
splinters into rough shards, tickling us to cough.

When I ask: 'How can you?'
A reply comes through curtain of smoke.

'Laughter is the same as crying,
only there are no tears.'

Reflexology

Beatings:

To the top of the head
elicit an idiot's smile.

To the ears and nape
affect your balance,

tipping you dangerously
close to insanity.

To the face humiliate you,
destroy perspective.

To the back, slash your
self confidence, invert your anger.

To the soles of your feet
erode your sense of humour.

To your stomach, exaggerate
your hunger and desire.

Beatings change you.
Drive a wedge between what is

essential and the husk that
haunts your old life, replying:

'I'm fine, and you?'

Solitaire

Lampblack smears my vision,

fading into 220 shades of grey concrete.
Yet I cannot tell

where the shadows end and I beg-
in your head

Voices

Visitations from seraphim

compensate for human absence.

Mantra

Angels stalk me in sleep.

I dream myself awake,

dreaming myself asleep.

I will build me a ladder,
wrestling eagles on every rung.

I will myself to live, so hard, until
the darkness crumbles, ash on my tongue.

Dream Stealers

Refuse to give in to it, the nothingness
       that smears ice on your soul,
          numbing life out.
Unlike Peters from Calabar who died after 2 days,

screaming: 'They stole everything!'

And they will if you let them:
       memories, dreams, hope.

Nirvana

Solitary
rolls sensuously off the tongue, whispering
hoarsely of Buddhas, hermits and nirvana.

Your spiritual dilemma?
3 days in wet or a month in dry.

Standing
stagnant green water breeds larvae
and bacteria up to your chest.

Sitting
is out of the question, unless you are
a fish; sleep is death. And not philosophically.

How many mosquito eggs can be laid in
4 square feet?

Dry solitary is not much better.
You stare at your hands alternating

between seamless darkness and spot
dancing fluorescent light.

Continuity
is impossible to maintain and time
becomes pores counted in your arm.

Moby Dick

Graffiti painted in excrement
on prison walls infects the very air,
burning nicotine-tan stains on our lungs:

FOLOW THE YELLO BRIK ROAD — CAPUTIN AHAB

Six Ways to Deal with It

1. Shut yourself away in your head, pretend it doesn't exist.

2. Punish yourself, blaming it on some fault in your own nature.

3. Scream down the dark corridors to insanity.

4. Lose yourself in its power, indulging in violence.

5. Break in its wake, crumbling to dust.

6. Join the others in the courtyard playing football.

Articles of Faith

Skills
learnt in prison are meant to
prepare you to assimilate on the outside,

But what to do with
a disciplined anus that can hide a
sharpened nail, piece of glass or even pencil?

How do you apply
the educated guesses; an ability
to predict who will live or die today?

Can you share or even tell
of philosophies and insights gleaned in
silent places of solitary confinement?

And who will buy
the blood you sold pint by pint to guards
in exchange for cigarettes, Coca-Cola or bread?

Your blood which they sold on to hospitals
private clinics, research facilities
and *obeah* men in *juju* shrines.

Who will believe
you can compose whole symphonies in your head
waiting the romance of strings and voices, because

here we are forbidden to sing?

Epiphany

An artist,
I
hang all hope for redemption
on ephemeral incandescent dreams.

Roping faith into filaments of light,
I climb on sunbeams
into the very eye of God.

Jacob's Ladder

Release, alive, from Kiri Kiri
is rare.

They hand you what is left of
your personal belongings

in a polythene bag. Everything
they did not want.

You step out and stand in the
sun thawing like a side of beef

from a freezer. Yet you are afraid
to proceed more than a few

steps from the gate. Convinced you
will be shot in the back,

or that people will recoil from you
knowing you carry the stench

of death on your now paler skin.
But nothing happens.

A gentle breeze ruffles your shirt and
a dog menaces a parked car.

The smell of frying plantain,
carried gently, hurts inexplicably.

Cold, sweet Coca-Cola stings you
to tears.

Postscripts – London

My tongue is heavy with new language
but I cannot give birth speech

Kamau Braithwaite
Eating the Dead

Postcard Pictures

1

Winter's sun is a sucked out lozenge
framed in the far window.

Before me a choice: Red to declare, Green not to.
But simple decisions consume me in panic.

Customs officers eye me with hostility
under neon lights that say: WELCOME TO LONDON
 HEATHROW.

I swallow the fear fisting my throat
but words are a meditation that eludes me.

2

Coffee percolates the arrival hall.
Signs jostle behind a barrier.
MR JONES, MR KOMOYOTO, SONY MUSIC REP.

I scan the patient group, shrinking.
Memories of prison – a not too distant past –
jelly my limbs.

Families buying their children's lives
from indifferent demons playing draughts
in the shade of the execution tree,

stand just outside the gates, holding
our gaze hoping to jog memories as we file past.
Names on signs, runes spelling

our future

and just as them,
I am terrified no one remembers me.
Then I am trembling on the cusp of a hug.

3

Hope is a fragile moth wing
unsure in the winter sun, clinging to
corners longing for night's muted light.

In the spaces between my belief,
cracks too old, too deep for anything
but terror,

contract, filling up with tinsel from
the still beating desperate wing sewn
to rear view mirror by a spiders web.

4

Chance is the random pen scratch of winning
LOTTO numbers, the casual flush hand, perfect dice roll.
an ability to conceive of brighter futures in clichéd
    hope,

the deliberate play of a chess piece
altering larger game plans
as chance computes a different trajectory.

Chance is the random smile, gummy
toothless and radiant, from my niece.

5

Grey walls weep grainy tears.
Police car passes me in the street.

Instinctively I hug the shadows,
indistinguishable as a dot on snowing TV.

Stitching darkness into a shroud,
I contain my fear like hair in a talisman

inhaling its acrid smell.
Comforted.

6

Winter rain washes blood
from streetlights into gutters,
icing the tip of my hair.

Snow, feather-light, falls
as bolls from a silk-cotton tree.
Yet seeds, orotund with

portents defying my fears;
a dragon swallowing the sun.

7

The middle-aged Indian woman,
sandwiched between boards advertising
West End shows she may never see,

haunts the fringes of Piccadilly Circus,
hugging warmth from a roast-chestnut vendor.
I imagine Kentucky Fried Chicken diffuses

her soft saffron and coriander scent,
breaking my heart even as her
still gentle eyes give me hope.

8

Victoria Line. Packed. People.
Sweat is the harbinger of other terror:

Small dark room stuffed too full
of desperate men; possibility falling away

with flakes of skin. Where pleasure is
an itch unscratched until the inevitability

is frenetic and love is a sharp cut
to jugular of those too sick to die.

Faith is a caterpillar nibbling
my fear to stalk brushing impotently.

Safe, knowing these doors will open, spilling
us at the next brightly lit station.

9

The policeman stops me on Kingsland High Street.
I resign myself to the cross, arms raised up.

'I see you know the routine,' he sneers.
My shame is a hot tear splattering

the cold metal of my saxophone, hissing
in the heat of his contempt.

10

When I first arrived,
everyone spoke of the Angel at Islington.

I went seeking redemption but found
only an old bum searching the bins outside Burger
    King.

And I was saved.

Things to Do in London When You Are Dead

1. Ride the Circle Line endlessly, chasing the dragon's tail.

2. Count the dots on your fuzzy television eating a late doner kebab.

3. Stand in the centre of Oxford Circus and scream. No matter. No one will see you.

4. Tell everyone you meet you are a poet. Someone will eventually put you out of your misery.

Field Song

Memory is a never-ending pain,
two by four catching your breath
in a sharp exhalation and you are
falling, falling, falling.

Tomorrow is almost a hope too much;
wishing-bone wish torn from chicken
and you are
praying, praying, praying.

Haunting

We return. The living.
Again. Wearing grief in gentle
bouquets, laid:

We return. The living.
Not the dead. Fast flitting shadows rifling
between mental gravestones trying
to fix a thing unbroken.

Easter Sunday

Will I turn fifty, still haunting
fading cafés, clutching my manuscript,
creased, stained and much commented on,
in dirty nailed hands
bumming bland too milky teas
off youngsters.
Charming them with my tales of
the establishment; rolled-up cigarette
half smoked, my life a continuity of middles,
ending inked out in the second draft.
Too afraid to even become an alcoholic.

Returning from Croydon

The train rolls over the Thames
where lights skate the uneven lap of water.

Gas towers are boils festering the skyline,
lanced by the trains running between.

A train going the opposite way holds
out the promise that life does not

go just one way, but
retraces its steps faithfully.

Babylon

Standing on Embankment bridge,
I search for the courage to jump
into the Thames sixty feet below.
The water is choppy and cold and my pockets are
heavy with guilt.

I've seen this on TV;
If the drop does not kill me
the cold will and if not that, there is
the pollution: fail safe, you see.

My grip on the wet railing slips and
my heart plummets first.
My fear is a howling, challenging the trains
screaming past behind me.

Dog's bark pulls my attention to its busking master.
An old rasta strumming a near-dead guitar,
its last two strings winding tenaciously onto life.

Face scarred by regret and too much living,
voice rough from so many tiny daily deaths,
eyes blind with need and the salty dissolving
aftertaste of faith:

There is a land far far away,
There is a land far across the sea, hey,
There is a land, where there's no night only day, hey,
There is a land, far far away, hey,

And his song is a gentle coaxing that pulls me
back from the abyss, tugging me tenderly
until I collapse at his feet, face buried in his dog's fur
sobbing brokenly.

Changing Times

'These are the days of miracles and wonder'

Paul Simon
Graceland

Three minute spaghetti. Boil in the bag fish.
Pot noodle. A mug of Batchelor's instant soup,

amaze me nearly as much as
microwaves, my new laptop and the

enduring power of Coltrane's *A Love Supreme*
and Miles' *Kind of Blue*.

It's not that I have lowered standards
with a too grateful palate

or that much espoused masculine
fascination for new toys and old jazz.

But I am learning to taste my life
without judgement. I think.

Days of Thunder

Celibate for five years –

except for that one time with
a prostitute, whose incessant chatter
about her son conspired with my Catholic
dread of Gomorrah to rob me of an erection.

Not a Love Song

Dreams stalk me and my cry
is a bird, wing broken.

Her gentle breathing beside me
is a warmth straining my terrors

into harmless biscuit crumbs
that I brush from the bed.

A Definition for Tomorrow

'If this is all I have
I can travel no further'

Kamau Braithwaite
Shepherd

There is a rumoured funk of damp earth

misting my friend's small garden. Snails
crunch underfoot as he leads me to where
his cat, Tiddles, was buried in a biscuit tin
six years before.

Huddling under a tree, sucking on a cigarette
he says: 'See, I know your loss.'
The future is the rough bark of that tree
rooted in my father's bones.